298.   25-

NEW POEMS

1962

ROBERT GRAVES
NEW POEMS
1962

CASSELL · LONDON

CASSELL & COMPANY LTD
35 Red Lion Square · London WC1
and at
MELBOURNE · SYDNEY · TORONTO
JOHANNESBURG · CAPE TOWN · AUCKLAND

© International Authors N.V. 1962
First published 1962

Printed by
Benham & Company Limited, Colchester
F.762

FOREWORD

Privacy finds herself a nook
In bold print of an open book
Which few have eyes to read; the rest
(If studiously inclined) will look
For cypher or for palimpsest.

The two parts of this book, like those of
More Poems 1961, are numbered as con-
tinuations of *Collected Poems 1959*.

R.G.

Deyá
Majorca

CONTENTS

XIII

XIV

XIII

RUBY AND AMETHYST

Two women: one as good as bread,
　　Bound to a sturdy husband.
Two women: one as rare as myrrh,
　　Bound only to herself.

Two women: one as good as bread,
　　Faithful to every promise.
Two women: one as rare as myrrh,
　　Who never pledges faith.

The one a flawless ruby wears
　　But with such innocent pleasure
A stranger's eye might think it glass
　　And take no closer look.

Two women: one as good as bread,
　　The noblest of the city.
Two women: one as rare as myrrh,
　　Who needs no public praise.

The pale rose-amethyst on her breast
　　Has such a garden in it
Your eye could wander there for hours,
　　And wonder, and be lost.

About her head a swallow wheels
　　Nor ever breaks the circuit:
Glory and awe of womanhood
　　Still undeclared to man.

Two women: one as good as bread,
Resistant to all weathers.
Two women: one as rare as myrrh,
Her weather still her own.

RECOGNITION

When on the cliffs we met, by chance,
    I startled at your quiet voice
And watched the swallows round you dance
    Like children that had made a choice.

Simple it was, as I stood there,
    To penetrate the mask you wore,
Your secret lineage to declare
    And your lost dignities restore.

Yet thus I earned a poet's fee
    So far out-distancing desire
That swallows yell in rage at me
    As who would set their world on fire.

VARIABLES OF GREEN

Grass-green and aspen-green,
Laurel-green and sea-green,
Fine-emerald-green,
And many another hue:
As green commands the variables of green
So love my many loves of you.

THE WATCH

Since the night in which you stole
    Like a phantom to my bed,
Seized my throat and from it wrung
    Vows that could not be unsaid:

Here beneath my arching ribs
    Red-hot embers, primed to be
Blown upon by winds of love,
    Scorch away mortality.

Like sledgehammers my two fists,
    My broad forehead grim with pride,
Muscles corded on my calves
    And my frame gigantified.

Yet your watching for an hour
    That our mutual stars will bless
Proves you more entranced than I
    Who go parched in hope of less.

NAME DAY

Tears of delight that on my name-day
She gave me nothing, and in return
Accepted every gift I heaped upon her—
Call me the richest poet alive!

UNCALENDARED LOVE

The first name cut on a rock, a King's,
Marked the beginning of time's annals;
And each new year would recapitulate
The unkind sloughings and renewals
Of the death-serpent's checkered coat.

But you with me together, together, together,
Survive ordeals never before endured:
We snatch the quill out of Enoch's hand
To obliterate our names from his black scroll—
Twin absentees of time.

Ours is uncalendared love, whole life,
As long or brief as befalls. Alone, together,
Recalling little, prophesying less,
We watch the serpent, crushed by your bare heel,
Rainbow his scales in a deathward agony.

THE MEETING

We, two elementals, woman and man,
Approached each other from far away:
I on the lower wind, she on the upper.

And the faith with which we came invested
By the blind thousands of our twin worlds
Formed thunder clouds about us.

Never such uproar as when we met,
Nor such forked lightning; rain in a cataract
Tumbled on deserts dry these thousand years.

What of the meteorologists?
They said nothing, turned their faces away,
Let the event pass unrecorded.

And what of us? We also said nothing.
Is it not the height of silent humour
To cause an unknown change in the earth's climate?

LACK

Born from ignoble stock on a day of dearth
He tramps the roads, trailing his withered branch,
And grudges every beauty of the wide earth.

Lack is his name, and although in gentleness
You set him honourably at the high table
And load his plate with luxury of excess,

Crying: 'Eat well, brother, and drink your fill,'
Yet with hunger whetted only, he boasts aloud:
'I have never begged a favour, nor ever will!'

His clothes are sad, but a burly wretch is he,
Of lustreless look, slack mouth, a borrowed wit,
And a sigh that would charm the song-bird from her tree.

Now he casts his eye in greed upon your demesne
With open mockery of a heart so open
It dares this gallows-climber to entertain.

NOT AT HOME

Her house loomed at the end of a Berkshire lane,
Tall but retired. She was expecting me;
And I approached with light heart and quick tread,
Having already seen from the garden gate
How bright her knocker shone—in readiness
For my confident rap?—and the steps holystoned.
I ran the last few paces, rapped and listened
Intently for the rustle of her approach. . . .

No reply, no movement. I waited three long minutes,
Then, in surprise, went down the path again
To observe the chimney stacks. No smoke from either.
And the curtains: were they drawn against the sun?
Or against what, then? I glanced over a wall
At her well-tended orchard, heavy with bloom
(Easter fell late that year, Spring had come early),
And found the gardener, bent over cold frames.

'Her ladyship is not at home?'
                                'No, sir.'
'She was expecting me. My name is Lion.
Did she leave a note?'
                        'No, sir, she left no note.'
'I trust nothing has happened . . . ?'
                                        'No, sir, nothing . . .
And yet she seemed preoccupied: we guess
Some family reason.'
                    '*Has* she a family?'
'That, sir, I could not say . . . She seemed distressed—
Not quite herself, if I may venture so.'

'But she left no note?'
                        'Only a verbal message:
Her ladyship will be away some weeks
Or months, hopes to return before midsummer,
And, please, you are not to communicate.
There was something else: about the need for patience.'

The sun went in, a bleak wind shook the blossom,
Dust flew, the windows glared in a blank row . . .
And yet I felt, when I turned slowly away,
Her eyes boring my back, as it might be posted
Behind a curtain slit, and still in love.

HORIZON

On a clear day how thin the horizon
Drawn between sea and sky,
Between sea-love and sky-love;
And after sunset how debatable
Even for an honest eye.

'Do as you will tonight,'
Said she, and so he did
By moonlight, candlelight,
Candlelight and moonlight,
While pillowed clouds the horizon hid.

Knowing-not-knowing that such deeds must end
In a curse that lovers long past weeping for
Had heaped upon him: she would be gone one night
With his familiar friend,
Granting him leave her beauty to explore
By moonlight, candlelight,
Candlelight and moonlight.

GOLDEN ANCHOR

Gone: and to an undisclosed region,
Free as the wind, if less predictable.
Why should I grieve, who have no claim on her?
My ring circles her finger, from her neck
Dangles my powerful jade. All is not lost
While still she wears those evident tokens
And no debts lie between us except love.

Or does the golden anchor plague her
As a drag on woman's liberty? Longing
To cut the cable, run grandly adrift,
Is she warned by a voice what wide misfortune
Ripples from ill faith?—therefore temporizes
And fears to use the axe, although consorting
With lovelessness and evil?

What should I say or do? It was she chose me,
Not contrariwise. Moreover, if I lavished
Extravagant praise on her, she deserved all.
I have been honest in love, as is my nature;
She secret, as is hers. I cannot grieve
Unless for having vexed her by unmasking
A jewelled virtue she was loth to use.

LION LOVER

You chose a lion to be your lover—
Me, who in joy such doom greeting
Dared jealously undertake
Cruel ordeals long foreseen and known,
Springing a trap baited with flesh: my own.

Nor would I now exchange this lion heart
For a less furious other,
Though by the Moon possessed
I gnaw at dry bones in a lost lair
And, when clouds cover her, roar my despair.

Gratitude and affection I disdain
As cheap in any market:
Your naked feet upon my scarred shoulders,
Your eyes naked with love,
Are all the gifts my beasthood can approve.

IBYCUS IN SAMOS

The women of Samos are lost in love for me:
Nag at their men, neglect their looms,
And send me secret missives, to my sorrow.

I am the poet Ibycus, known by the cranes,
Each slender Samian offers herself moon-blanched
As my only bride, my heart's belovèd;

And when I return a calm salute, no more,
Or a brotherly kiss, will heap curses upon me:
Do I despise her warm myrrh-scented bosom?

She whom I honour has turned her face away
A whole year now, and in pride more than royal
Lacerates my heart and hers as one.

Wherever I wander in this day-long fever,
Sprigs of the olive-trees are touched with fire
And stones twinkle along my devious path.

Who here can blame me if I alone am poet,
If none other has dared to accept the fate
Of death and again death in the Muse's house?

Or who can blame me if my hair crackles
Like thorns under a pot, if my eyes flash
As it were sheets of summer lightning?

POSSESSED

To be possessed by her is to possess—
Though rooted in this thought
Build nothing on it.

Unreasonable faith becomes you
And mute endurance
Even of betrayal.

Never expect to be brought wholly
Into her confidence.
Being natural woman

She knows what she must do, not why;
Balks your anticipation
Of pleasure vowed;

Yet, no less vulnerable than you,
Suffers the dire pangs
Of your self-defeat.

THE WINGED HEART

Trying to read the news, after your visit,
When the words made little sense, I let them go;
And found my heart suddenly sprouting feathers.

Alone in the house, and the full honest rain
After a devil's own four-day sirocco
Still driving down in sheets across the valley—

How it hissed, how the leaves of the olives shook!
We had suffered drought since earliest April;
Here we were already in October.

I have nothing more to tell you. What has been said
Can never possibly be retracted now
Without denial of the large universe.

Some curse had fallen between us, a dead hand,
An inhalation of evil sucking up virtue:
Which left us no recourse, unless we turned

Improvident as at our first encounter,
Deriding practical care of how or where:
Your certitude must be my certitude.

And the tranquil blaze of sky etherializing
The circle of rocks and our own rain-wet faces,
Was that not worth a lifetime of pure grief?

IN TRANCE AT A DISTANCE

It is easy, often, and natural even,
To commune with her in trance at a distance;
To attest those deep confessionary sighs
Otherwise so seldom heard from her;
To be assured by a single shudder
Wracking both hearts, and underneath the press
Of clothes by a common nakedness.

Hold fast to the memory, lest a cold fear
Of never again here, of nothing good coming,
Should lure you into self-delusive trade
With demonesses who dare masquerade
As herself in your dreams, and who after awhile
Skilfully imitate her dancing gait,
Borrow her voice and vocables and smile.

It is no longer—was it ever?—in your power
To catch her close to you at any hour:
She has raised a wall of nothingness in between
(Were it something known and seen, to be torn apart,
You could grind its heartless fragments into the ground);
Yet, taken in trance, would she still deny
That you are hers, she yours, till both shall die?

THE WREATH

A bitter year it was. What woman ever
Cared for me so, yet so ill-used me,
Came in so close and drew so far away,
So much promised and performed so little,
So murderously her own love dared betray?
Since I can never be clear out of your debt,
Queen of ingratitude, to my dying day,
You shall be punished with a deathless crown
For your dark head, resist it how you may.

IN HER PRAISE

This they know well: the Goddess yet abides.
Though each new lovely woman whom she rides,
Straddling her neck a year or two or three,
Should sink beneath such weight of majesty
And, groping back to humankind, gainsay
The headlong power that whitened all her way
With a broad track of trefoil—leaving you,
Her chosen lover, ever again thrust through
With daggers, your purse rifled, your rings gone—
Nevertheless they call you to live on
To parley with the pure, oracular dead,
To hear the wild pack whimpering overhead,
To watch the moon tugging at her cold tides.
Woman is mortal woman. She abides.

THE ALABASTER THRONE

This tall lithe Amazon armed herself
With all the cunning of a peasant father
Who, fled to Corinth from starved Taenarum,
Had cherished her, the child of his new wealth,
Almost as though a son.

From Corinth she embarked for Paphos
Where white doves, circling, settled on her palms
And a sudden inspiration drew us
To heap that lap with pearls, almost as though
Ignorant of her antecedents.

Which was the Goddess, which the woman?
Let the philosophers break their teeth on it!
She had seized an empty alabaster throne
And for two summers, almost, could deny
Both Taenarum and Corinth.

A RESTLESS GHOST

Alas for obstinate doubt: the dread
Of error in supposing my heart freed,
All care for her stone dead!
Ineffably will shine the hills and radiant coast
Of early morning when she is gone indeed,
Her divine elements disbanded, disembodied
And through the misty orchards in love spread—
When she is gone indeed—
But still among them moves her restless ghost.

BETWEEN MOON AND MOON

In the last sad watches of night
Hardly a sliver of light will remain
To edge the guilty shadow of a waned moon
That dawn must soon devour.

                    Thereafter, another
Crescent queen shall arise with power—
So wise a beauty never yet seen, say I:
A true creature of moon, though not the same
In nature, name or feature—
Her innocent eye rebuking inconstancy
As if Time itself should die and disappear.

So was it ever. She is here again, I sigh.

BEWARE, MADAM!

Beware, madam, of the witty devil,
The arch intriguer who walks disguised
In a poet's cloak, his gay tongue oozing evil.

Would you be a Muse? He will so declare you,
Pledging his blind allegiance,
Yet remain secret and uncommitted.

Poets are men: are single-hearted lovers
Who adore and trust beyond all reason,
Who die honourably at the gates of hell.

The Muse alone is licensed to do murder
And to betray: weeping with honest tears
She thrones each victim in her paradise.

But from this Muse the devil borrows an art
That ill becomes a man. Beware, madam:
He plots to strip you bare of woman-pride.

He is capable of seducing your twin-sister
On the same pillow, and neither she nor you
Will suspect the act, so close a glamour he sheds.

Alas, being honourably single-hearted,
You adore and trust beyond all reason,
Being no more a Muse than he a poet.

THE CLIFF EDGE

Violence threatens you no longer:
It was your innocent temerity
Caused us to tremble: veterans discharged
From the dirty wars of life.

Forgive us this presumption: we are abashed—
As when a child, straying on the cliff's edge,
Turns about to ask her white-faced brothers:
'Do you take me for a child?'

THE MILLER'S MAN

The imperturbable miller's man
Whose help the boy implored, drowning,
Drifting slowly past the mill,
Was a stout swimmer, yet would not come between
The river-god and his assured victim.

Soon he too, swimming in the sun,
Is caught with cramp; and the boy's ghost
Jeers from the reeds and rushes.
But he drowns valiantly in silence,
This being no one's business but his own.

Let us not reckon the miller's man
With Judas or with Jesus,
But with the cattle, who endure all weathers,
Or with the mill-wheel foolishly creaking,
Incurious of the grain in the bins.

ACROBATS

Poised impossibly on the high tight-rope
    Of love, in spite of all,
They still preserve their dizzying balance
And smile this way or that,
    As though uncertain on which side to fall.

OUZO UNCLOUDED

Here is ouzo (she said) to try you:
Better not drowned in water,
Better not chilled with ice,
Not sipped at thoughtfully,
Nor toped in secret.
Drink it down (she said) unclouded
At a blow, this tall glass full,
But keep your eyes on mine
Like a true Arcadian acorn-eater.

THE BROKEN GIRTH

Bravely from Fairyland he rode, on furlough,
Astride a tall bay given him by the Queen
From whose couch he had leaped not a half-hour since,
Whose lilies-of-the-valley shone from his helm.

But alas, as he paused to assist five Ulstermen
Sweating to raise a recumbent Ogham pillar,
Breach of a saddle-girth tumbled Oisín
To common Irish earth. And at once, it is said,
Old age came on him with grief and frailty.

St. Patrick asked: would he not confess the Christ?—
Which for that Lady's sake he loathed to do,
But northward loyally turned his eyes in death.
It was Fenians bore the unshriven corpse away
For burial, keening.
                            Curse me all squint-eyed monks
Who misconstrue the passing of Finn's son:
Old age, not Fairyland, was his delusion.

INKIDOO AND THE QUEEN OF BABEL

When I was a callant, born far hence,
You first laid hand on my innocence,
But sent your champion into a boar
That my fair young body a-pieces tore.

When I was a lapwing, crowned with gold,
Your lust and liking for me you told,
But plucked my feathers and broke my wing—
Wherefore all summer for grief I sing.

When I was a lion of tawny fell,
You stroked my mane and you combed it well,
But pitfalls seven you dug for me
That from one or other I might not flee.

When I was a courser, proud and strong,
That like the wind would wallop along,
You bated my pride with spur and bit
And many a rod on my shoulder split.

When I was a shepherd that for your sake
The bread of love at my hearth would bake,
A ravening wolf did you make of me
To be thrust from home by my brothers three.

When I tended your father's orchard close
I brought you plum, pear, apple and rose,
But my lusty manhood away you stole
And changed me into a grovelling mole.

When I was simple, when I was fond,
Thrice and thrice did you wave your wand,
But now you vow to be leal and true
And softly ask, will I wed with you?

THREE SONGS FOR THE LUTE

I

TRUTH IS POOR PHYSIC

A wild beast falling sick
Will find his own best physic—
    Herb, berry, root of tree
Or wholesome salt to lick—
    And so run free.

But this I know at least
Better than a wild beast:
    That should I fall love-sick
And the wind veer to East,
    Truth is poor physic.

II

IN HER ONLY WAY

When her need for you dies
    And she wanders apart,
Never rhetoricize
    On the faithless heart.

But with manlier virtue
    Be content to say
She both loved you and hurt you
    In her only way.

III

HEDGES FREAKED WITH SNOW

No argument, no anger, no remorse,
　　No dividing of blame.
There was poison in the cup—why should we ask
　　From whose hand it came?

No grief for our dead love, no howling gales
　　That through darkness blow,
But the smile of sorrow, a wan winter landscape,
　　Hedges freaked with snow.

THE AMBROSIA OF DIONYSUS AND SEMELE

Little slender lad, toad-headed,
For whom ages and leagues are dice to throw with,
Smile back to where entranced I wander
Gorged with your bitter flesh,
Drunk with your Virgin Mother's lullaby.

Little slender lad, lightning engendered,
Grand master of magicians:
When pirates stole you at Icaria
Wild ivy gripped their rigging, every oar
Changed to a serpent, panthers held the poop,
A giant vine sprouted from the mast crotch
And overboard they plunged, the whey-faced crew!

Lead us with your song, tall Queen of earth!
Twinned to the god, I follow comradely
Through a first rainbow-limbo, webbed in white,
Through chill Tyrrhenian grottoes, under water,
Where dolphins wallow between marble rocks,
Through sword-bright jungles, tangles of unease,
Through halls of fear ceilinged with incubi,
Through blazing treasure-chambers walled with garnet,
Through domes pillared with naked Caryatids—
Then mount at last on wings into pure air,
Peering down with regal eye upon
Five-fruited orchards of Elysium,
In perfect knowledge of all knowledges.

And still she drowsily chants
From her invisible bower of stars.
Gentle her voice, her notes come linked together
In intricate golden chains paid out
Slowly across brocaded cramoisy,
Or unfold like leaves from the jade-green shoot
Of a rising bush whose blossoms are her tears. . . .
O, whenever she pauses, my heart quails
Until the sound renews.

Little slender lad, little secret god,
Pledge her your faith in me,
Who have ambrosia eaten and yet live.

THE UNNAMED SPELL

Let us never name that royal certitude,
That simultaneous recognition
When first we stood together,

When I saw you as a child astonished,
Years before, under tall trees
By a marching sound of wind:

Your heart sown with a headlong wisdom
Which every grief or joy thereafter
Rooted still more strongly.

Naming is treacherous, names divide
Truth into lesser truths, enclosing them
In a coffin of counters—

Give the spell no name, liken it only
To the more than tree luxuriating
Seven ells above the earth:

All heal, golden surprise of a kiss,
Wakeful glory while the grove winters,
A branch Hell-harrowing,

Of no discoverable parentage,
Strangeling scion of varied stocks
Yet true to its own leaf,

Secret of secrets disclosed only
To who already share it,
Who themselves have sometime raised an arch—
Pillared with honour; its lintel, love—
And passed silently through.